The ELI Readers collection is a co...
range of books and plays for readers
of all ages, ranging from captivating
contemporary stories to timeless classics.
There are three series, each catering for
a different age group; Young ELI Readers,
Teen ELI Readers and Young Adult ELI
Readers. The books are carefully edited
and beautifully illustrated to capture the
essence of the stories and plots.
The readers are supplemented with
'Focus on' texts packed with background
cultural information about the writers and
their lives and times.

Charles Dickens

# A Christmas Carol

Adaptation and Activities by Elizabeth Ferretti
Illustrated by Veronica Ruffato

YOUNG ADULT ELI READERS

Charles Dickens
**A Christmas Carol**
Adaptation and activities by Elizabeth Ferretti
Language Level Consultant: Lisa Suett
Illustrated by Veronica Ruffato

**ELI Readers**
**Founder and Series Editors**
Paola Accattoli, Grazia Ancillani, Daniele Garbuglia (Art Director)

**Graphic Design**
Airone Comunicazione - Sergio Elisei

**Layout**
Airone Comunicazione

**Production Manager**
Francesco Capitano

**Photo credits**
Shutterstock, ELI Archive

© 2017 ELI s.r.l.
P.O. Box 6
62019 Recanati MC
Italy
T +39 071750701
F +39 071977851
info@elionline.com
www.elionline.com

Typeset in 11,5 / 15 pt Monotype Dante

Printed in Italy by Tecnostampa – Pigini Group Printing Division –
Loreto – Trevi (Italia) – ERA332.01
ISBN 978-88-536-2317-1

First edition: March 2017

**www.eligradedreaders.com**

# Contents

These icons indicate the parts of the story that are recorded

start ▶    stop ■

# MAIN CHARACTERS

Ebenezer
Scrooge

Fred and his wife

Bob Cratchit

Tiny Tim

The Ghost
of Christmas Past

Jacob
Marley

The Ghost
of Christmas Present

The Ghost
of Christmas Yet to Come

# Vocabulary

**1a** **Read the letter.**

> Marley & Scrooge
> Financial Services
> Finch Lane
> City of London
>
> Mr Arthur Mackie
> 23, Bayham Street
> Camden Town
> North London
>
> 23rd December, 1843
>
> Dear Sir,
>
> I write to remind you that on 26th December you must pay
> me the money you borrowed, and 50% extra for my costs.
> I have an office to pay for and a clerk who expects to have
> a fire to keep him warm. I can't give you money for nothing!
> I don't want to hear excuses – I've heard them all before.
> 'I broke my leg and can't work', 'I don't have a job', 'My wife
> is dying'. People take too long to die in my opinion.
> I'm an old man, but I'm not stupid. Jacob Marley and I did
> not start this business to help lazy people. There is always
> room for people like you in the prisons of London.
>
> Yours,
> Ebenezer Scrooge

## 1b Now answer the questions.

**1** Which of the following phrases best describes Ebenezer Scrooge?
- **A** ☐ as hard as stone
- **B** ☐ warm and caring
- **C** ☐ a good man of business

**2** In England in 1843, what can happen to people if they can't pay back money they've borrowed?
- **A** ☐ they can ask for help
- **B** ☐ businesses wait until they can pay
- **C** ☐ they could go to prison

**3** Which phrase best describes what Ebenezer Scrooge thinks about poor people?
- **A** ☐ they are bad people
- **B** ☐ they don't try hard enough
- **C** ☐ they have been unlucky

## 2 Complete these sentences.

**1** In 1843 people lit their homes and offices with
- **A** ☐ candles and oil lamps
- **B** ☐ one electric light per house
- **C** ☐ only natural light

**2** In London at this time, people heated their homes and offices with
- **A** ☐ the heat of the sun
- **B** ☐ fires (using wood, for example)
- **C** ☐ gas fires

**3** In London in 1843, most people moved about the city
- **A** ☐ by bicycle
- **B** ☐ by horse
- **C** ☐ on foot or in 'buses' pulled by horses

## 3 Describe how you celebrate Christmas or other important holidays with your family and friends.

_____

_____

_____

Chapter 1

# Jacob Marley

▶ 2  Jacob Marley was dead. He was definitely dead. The priest and the man who had prepared the body, the church clerk and Scrooge had all signed the official document to say he was dead. Scrooge's name was worth a lot on a document – the men who worked in the businesses and banks of the City of London respected that name.

Did Scrooge know for sure that he was dead? Of course he did. How could he not know? Ebenezer Scrooge and Jacob Marley had been business partners for many years. He organised everything after Marley died and Scrooge was the only person who went to the church when he was buried. But even Scrooge was not upset by the death of his friend, and carried on working after he got back from church.

So, we can be absolutely sure that Marley was dead. This fact must be understood or nothing wonderful will come from this story I am going to tell you.

Years passed, but Scrooge did not take Marley's name from his office door. People called him Scrooge or Marley but he didn't correct them, he answered to both names.

People borrowed money from Scrooge but he always got every bit back, and more – they paid him extra so that they could borrow money from him. He was as hard as a stone, as sharp as a knife. He

didn't care if it was hard for people to pay him back. He loved money so much that he never let go of it.

His hair and eyebrows were white like ice. The cold within him froze his old nose, took the life out of his cheeks, turned his legs to wood, made his eyes red and his thin lips blue and it spoke in his high, cold voice.

He carried his own low temperature around with him – during the hottest days of summer, his office was icy.

Nobody stopped him in the street with a smile to say 'My dear Scrooge, how are you?' No homeless man or woman ever asked him for money, no children asked him what the time was, no one asked for directions, even the dogs of blind men took their owners out of Scrooge's path. Scrooge didn't care! He liked to be alone.

Once upon a time, then, on that good day of the year, Christmas Eve, Scrooge sat in his office adding up money in a large book. It was cold and foggy. Although it was only three o'clock in the afternoon, it was already dark. The door of Scrooge's room was open so that he could keep an eye on his clerk, who sat in a tiny little room copying letters. Scrooge had a very small fire, but his clerk's fire was even smaller. Every time the clerk wanted to make his fire bigger, Scrooge said he thought he would look for another clerk. So, the clerk put on his long white scarf and tried to warm himself by his candle, but he didn't have much imagination and he stayed as cold as before.

'A Merry* Christmas Uncle! God bless you*!' said a happy voice. It was Scrooge's nephew.

'Bah!' said Scrooge, 'Humbug*!'

Scrooge's nephew had walked so fast through the fog and freezing air that his handsome face was red and warm.

---

**merry** (mainly used in 'Merry Christmas') happy
**God bless (you)** ask God to take care of someone

**humbug** (not often used in modern English) false, not honest or real

'Christmas a humbug, Uncle?' said Scrooge's nephew. 'You don't mean that!'

'I do,' said Scrooge. 'Merry Christmas! What reason do you have to be merry? You're poor enough.'

'Come then,' his nephew answered happily, 'what reason do you have to be so cross? You're rich enough.'

'Of course I am cross, when I live in a world filled with fools. What is Christmas but a time for paying bills without money, a time for finding yourself a year older and not an hour richer? If I had my way, I would boil every fool who says Merry Christmas with his own Christmas pudding* and I would bury him with a branch of holly* through his heart!'

'Uncle! But Christmas is a time when people are kind, we forgive each other, we help those who have less than us *and* we enjoy ourselves. It's the only time in the whole year when men and women open their closed hearts to those around them. And so, while Christmas has never put any money in my pocket, it *has* done me good and *will* do me good!'

The clerk stood and clapped when he heard these words. Then he remembered this was not a good thing to do in front of Scrooge.

'If I hear another sound from *you*,' said Scrooge, 'you will celebrate Christmas by losing your job!' Then he turned to his nephew, 'You are quite a powerful speaker, sir. I am surprised you don't become a politician!'

'Don't be cross, Uncle. Will you have dinner with us tomorrow?'

Scrooge said something very rude at that.

'But why, Uncle? I want nothing from you, I ask nothing of you, why can't we be friends?'

---

**Christmas pudding** sweet food made with sugar, flour, dried fruit and fat, which is often boiled to cook it

**holly** small tree which has dark green leaves all year and red berries in winter

'Good afternoon,' Scrooge said, to tell his nephew the conversation was finished.

'I am sorry with all my heart to find you so difficult. But I won't let you make me unhappy, so a Merry Christmas, Uncle!'

'Good afternoon!' said Scrooge.

'And a Happy New Year!'

'Good afternoon!' said Scrooge.

His nephew left the room without an angry word, but before the clerk could close the door, two large and pleasant gentlemen came in.

'Do we have the pleasure of speaking with Mr Marley or Mr Scrooge?' one of them asked with a smile.

'Mr Marley has been dead these seven years,' Scrooge replied. 'He died exactly seven years ago tonight.'

'This is the time of year when we think about people who have less than us,' the man continued, not worried by Scrooge's face.

'Are there no prisons for them to go to?' interrupted Scrooge. 'And the poorhouses*? Do they still exist?

'Unfortunately, these bad places still exist,' the man said sadly.

'I am very glad to hear it,' said Scrooge. 'I shall give you nothing. Now, gentlemen, I wish to be left alone. I don't celebrate Christmas and I don't have enough money to make lazy people merry.'

'But the poorhouses are terrible,' said the first man, 'people would rather die than end their lives there!'

'If they would rather die, why don't they? And they should die quickly, then we wouldn't have so many people to feed! Good afternoon, gentlemen!'

---

**poorhouses** place where poor people could live in Victorian England

After they had gone, there was the sound of singing from the street. A boy was singing a Christmas carol* outside the door. Scrooge took a book from his desk and threw it at the door and the singing immediately stopped. The boy was singing for money and Scrooge certainly didn't want to give him any!

When the end of the day arrived, Scrooge stood up.

'I suppose you will want all of tomorrow off?' Scrooge asked.

'If that will not be a problem for you, sir?'

'Of course it's a problem,' said Scrooge, 'and it's not fair. I have to pay you for a day when you're not working!'

The clerk said that it was only once a year.

'But you are still taking money from my pocket! Be here extra early the next day.'

The clerk ran out into the streets and played in the snow with some children, before running home to Camden Town to his young family.

Scrooge went to the small restaurant where every night he ate his dinner. He read the papers and then walked home.

When he arrived at his front door, he saw something strange. The door seemed to have a face on it which looked like his old partner Marley, a strange, dead face. Scrooge shook his head and the face disappeared.

Scrooge was not easily frightened but when he went inside, he checked behind the door. There was no one. He checked everywhere but there was no one in the house. Most of the rooms were used as offices and they were shut now. Scrooge went up the stairs to his rooms. He closed the door and locked it twice, which he never did normally.

**carol** special Christmas song

Scrooge sat close to a small fire which had pictures round it to make it pretty. Scrooge thought he saw Marley's face in these pictures, but when he looked again, there was nothing strange about them.

'Humbug!' he said, but then his eyes were attracted to a large bell* that hung on the wall. He watched with growing fear as the bell began to move, softly at first and then more and more until it began to ring. Soon all the bells in the house were ringing.

This might have lasted for half a minute or a minute, but it seemed like an hour. Then, as suddenly as they had started, the bells stopped ringing. Then, from the bottom of the house he heard the noise of metal, like a chain pulled along the floor. The noise moved across the hall and up the stairs, getting closer and closer.

'It's humbug!' said Scrooge, 'I won't believe it!'

His colour changed though when it came through the locked door and into the room.

The same face, the very same. Marley with his hair tied back, Marley's shirt and coat. He was pulling a chain that was wrapped around his middle. The chain was made (Scrooge looked at it closely) of money boxes, keys, locks and metal purses.

Scrooge still did not believe what he saw. Although the ghost stood before him, although he felt its death-cold eyes and saw the cloth wrapped round its head, he still did not believe his eyes.

'What do you want with me?' asked Scrooge, cold and angry, 'Who are you?'

'Ask me who I *was*,' the ghost said.

'Who *were* you then?'

'In life, I was your partner, Jacob Marley.'

bell

# Comprehension

**1** **Complete these sentences with one or more details from the text.**

**1** People borrow money from Ebenezer Scrooge and he always gets _____

**2** Ebenezer Scrooge is a cold, old man with white hair and

_____

**3** When Scrooge walks through the streets, no one

_____

**4** When Scrooge's clerk tries to make his fire bigger, Scrooge says _____

**5** ...so the clerk _____

**6** Scrooge's nephew comes in to Scrooge's office to

_____

**7** Scrooge doesn't want to have dinner with his nephew and says that anyone who says 'Merry Christmas'

_____

**8** When two gentlemen come to ask for money to help the poor, Scrooge doesn't give them any because

_____

# Grammar

**2** **Make these phrases into questions**

**1** Scrooge knew that Marley was dead.

_____?

**2** You don't mean that, Uncle!

_____?

**3** I think you should become a politician!
(*Be careful!*) _____?

**4** I came to ask you to have dinner with us.

_____?

**3** Use the phrases below to make hypothetical sentences. The first one has been done as an example.

**0** borrowed money from Scrooge | pay every bit back.
*If you borrowed money from Scrooge, (then) you had to pay every bit back.*

**1** called him Marley | didn't correct them.
_____

**2** had my way | boil every fool who says 'Merry Christmas' with his own pudding.
_____

**3** hear another sound from you | celebrate Christmas by losing your job!
_____

**4** rather die | die quickly.
_____

# Speaking

**4** Read these questions, then discuss in pairs.

**1** If you were Scrooge's nephew, would you visit your uncle?
**2** If you were Scrooge's clerk, would you start looking for another job?

## PRE-READING ACTIVITY

**5a** Answer the following questions.

**1** If a ghost arrived in your sitting room, would you believe it was 'real'?
**2** Would you ask it to sit down?
**3** How would you feel if the ghost made a terrible noise?

▶3 **5b** Now listen to the first part of Chapter 2 – how would Scrooge answer the questions above?

Chapter 2

# The Ghost
of Christmas Past

▶ 3 Can you – can you sit down?' Scrooge asked Jacob Marley's ghost. He
wasn't sure if ghosts could sit on chairs. It could be embarrassing if
the ghost had to explain why.

'I can,' said the ghost.

'Then do it.'

The ghost sat down on the opposite side of the fire as if it sat there
every day.

'You don't believe in me,' said the ghost.

'I don't.'

'Why don't you believe what you see and hear?'

'I'm only seeing you because I had a badly cooked dinner. You
might be a bit of meat that is still sitting in my stomach, or a bit of
undercooked potato making me see what is not there!'

Scrooge did not often try to be funny, but he was extremely
frightened. Talking in this silly way made him less scared of the ghost's
voice, which terrified him down to his bones. There was another thing,
too. The ghost's hair and clothes were moving about as if they were
in the air from a hot oven, although Scrooge could not feel any heat.

'You see this?' asked Scrooge, holding up a dry biscuit he had
prepared for his supper.

'I do,' said the ghost, looking ahead.

'Well, if I eat this and it makes me ill, I might see a crowd of ghosts for the rest of my life. Humbug, I tell you – humbug!'

When it heard this, the ghost gave a terrible cry and shook its chain so loudly that Scrooge held tight onto his seat to stop himself falling down with fear. Then something really horrible happened. The ghost had a cloth wrapped round his head, and he started to unwrap it. As he took it off, the lower part of its face dropped down to below its shoulders. It was terrifying!

Scrooge was so frightened that he fell on his knees and raised his hands. 'Ghost, why do you trouble me?'

'I see you believe in me now,' it said.

'I do,' said Scrooge, 'but why do ghosts walk the earth?'

'I did nothing to make anyone happy when I was alive. Now, I must travel through the world to watch from a distance all the things I could have done when I was alive.'

The ghost cried out and shook his chain.

'And what is that chain?' asked Scrooge.

'I made this chain when I was alive. I made it piece by piece. I chose to make it and I chose to wear it because of how I lived my life. Don't you recognise it?'

Scrooge became very frightened.

'Would you like to know the weight and length of *your* chain?' asked the ghost. 'When I died, your chain was as heavy as this one, and seven years have passed since then.'

Scrooge looked around, but he couldn't see his own chain.

'Jacob!' Scrooge said, 'Tell me this isn't true!'

'I cannot. I will soon have to leave you. I have travelled without rest for seven years thinking about my life, but it's too late now. I can't change anything.'

'But you were always a good man of business,' said Scrooge.

'Business!' cried the ghost, 'The people around me were my business. I should have helped them! Instead, I walked with my eyes down, not seeing the poor homes where I could have helped.'

Scrooge was upset to hear the ghost speak like this.

'I don't understand how you see me tonight. I have sat next to you on many days,' the ghost continued.

Scrooge didn't like that idea.

'I have come to warn you. I am giving you the chance to escape what I've become,' the ghost said.

'You've always been a good friend to me, Jacob.'

'Three ghosts will come to visit you.'

'I'd rather they didn't,' said Scrooge.

'Expect the first tomorrow at one in the morning, the second will come on the next night at the same time. The third will come the next night when the bells ring midnight. I must go. Remember what I have told you.'

It started to walk backwards and as it walked the window opened. Outside the air was full of ghosts flying about, crying and talking unhappily. Scrooge recognised some of them. Then Marley was gone.

Scrooge tried to say 'Humbug!' but stopped at 'Hum'.

When Scrooge woke it was so dark he couldn't see anything out of the window. The heavy bell of the church clock started to ring 12. He

counted each ring, and it was a shock when it stopped at 12. He thought over and over about Jacob Marley. The more he thought, the more he didn't understand. He decided it had all been a dream, but as soon as he had decided that he started to question, 'Was it a dream or not?'

Outside, the clock rang one.

'It's one o'clock!' said Scrooge, 'And nothing has come!'

There were curtains all round Scrooge's bed to keep him warm. At the moment that the clock rang one, a hand opened the curtains right next to his head. Scrooge found himself face to face with a visitor from another world. It had a strange face, like a child, but not like a child, more like an old man. Its hair was long and hung down its back and was very white, but its skin was soft and pink like a baby's. The arms were long and strong, the hands and fingers were the same. It had on a white dress with a shining belt. It carried a piece of green holly, but round the edges of its dress were summer flowers. The strangest thing was a bright light that shone from the top of his head.

'Are you the ghost that Marley told me about?' asked Scrooge.

'I am!'

The voice was soft and gentle.

'Who, and what are you?' Scrooge asked.

'I am the Ghost of Christmas Past.'

'Long past?'

'No. Your past.'

Scrooge bravely asked what it was there for.

'To help save you.'

It put out its hand and took him gently by the arm.

'Get out of bed and walk with me!'

Scrooge knew it would make no difference if he told the ghost it was too late to go out, or that the weather, being so very cold, was not the best for going on a walk, or that the bed was warm and the temperature outside was freezing. The hand held his arm gently but when it pulled, Scrooge could not stop it. He got out of bed and the ghost took him towards the window. Scrooge asked him to stop.

'I'm a living person, not a ghost!' he said. 'I'll fall if I step out of the window!'

The ghost touched his heart. 'When I touch here, you won't have to worry about falling.'

The ghost and Scrooge walked through the wall and stood on a country road. London was gone. The darkness and the fog had also gone. It was a clear, cold, winter day with snow on the ground.

'I can hardly believe it!' said Scrooge, holding his hands together, and looking about him. 'I was a boy in this place!'

Scrooge smelled a thousand smells in the air, and with each smell he remembered a thousand thoughts and hopes, moments of happiness and sadness that he had forgotten about.

The ghost looked at him.

'You're crying,' it said.

Scrooge said it was nothing, he had something in his eye. He told the ghost to take him where it wanted.

'Do you remember the way?' the ghost asked.

'Remember it!' said Scrooge, 'I could walk it with my eyes shut!'

'It's strange, then, that you have forgotten it for so many years!' said the ghost, 'Let us go on.'

They walked along the road until a small town appeared. Scrooge recognised every gate and every tree on the way.

Some boys riding small horses were coming towards them. They were calling to other boys being taken home by their fathers. The boys were wonderfully happy, the road was full of merry music and the cold air laughed to hear it.

'These are shadows of things that have happened,' explained the ghost. 'They don't know that we're here.'

As the boys rode past, Scrooge knew them all and told the ghost their names excitedly. Why was he so happy to see them? Why did he love hearing them call out 'Merry Christmas' to each other as they took the road home? What was Merry Christmas to Scrooge?

'The school is not quite empty,' the ghost said. 'There's one child left there on his own.'

Scrooge knew who that was, and he was sad again.

They left the main road and walked up to a large, old house. The ghost and Scrooge went through the front door and across the hall, to a door which opened by itself onto a long, sad room with rows of desks and seats in it. On one of these seats, a lonely boy sat by a small fire, lost in a story book. Scrooge sat at a desk and cried to see his poor, forgotten self as he had been.

The ghost touched him on the arm and pointed*. Suddenly, they saw a man in foreign clothes standing outside the window.

'That's Ali Baba*!' said Scrooge with a smile. 'It's dear, honest Ali Baba!'

---

**point** put one finger out straight in the direction that you want someone to look

**Ali Baba** character from traditional Arab stories

Scrooge told the ghost all about Ali Baba and his adventures in a voice that was half way between crying and laughing. Scrooge's business friends in London would have been surprised to see him like this!

Then he said, 'Poor boy! I wish,' said Scrooge, putting his hand in his pocket, 'but it's too late now.'

'What is the matter?' asked the ghost.

'Nothing, nothing. There was a boy singing a Christmas carol at my door last night. I would like to give him something, that is all.'

The ghost smiled. 'Let's see another Christmas,' the ghost said. At that moment, the boy became a young man. He was walking up and down the room looking terribly sad.

Suddenly, the door opened. A little girl came running over to him.

'Dear, dear brother, I've come to bring you home! Father is much kinder now. He says you can come home to stay forever!'

'Home, little Fan?' the young Scrooge said.

'Yes! We'll spend Christmas together and have the happiest time in the whole world!'

When they got to the front door, the owner of the school told a man to bring Mr Scrooge's things, and Scrooge and his sister went home together.

'She was always such a small child. You felt the wind might blow her away,' the ghost said to old Scrooge, 'but she had a large heart.'

'You're right!' said Scrooge.

'She died when she was a woman and had children, I think.'

'One child,' Scrooge corrected the ghost.

'True,' said the ghost, 'your nephew!'

# Comprehension

**1** **What is the right answer, A, B, or C?**

**1** Scrooge said he was seeing the ghost because
   **A** ☐ he didn't believe in him.
   **B** ☐ he'd had a badly cooked dinner.
   **C** ☐ he was trying to be funny.

**2** The ghost gave a terrible cry and shook its chain so that
   **A** ☐ Scrooge would listen to what it was saying.
   **B** ☐ Scrooge would stop talking about his dinner.
   **C** ☐ Scrooge would believe that it was real.

**3** The ghost tells Scrooge that it had to carry the chain because
   **A** ☐ it hadn't been kind to people when it was alive.
   **B** ☐ all ghosts get one, including Scrooge.
   **C** ☐ it was heavy and it had to travel.

**4** Jacob Marley tells Scrooge that when he was alive he should have
   **A** ☐ walked past the poor.
   **B** ☐ looked after people and been patient with them.
   **C** ☐ warned Scrooge.

**5** The Ghost of Christmas Past has come to show Scrooge
   **A** ☐ that if he steps out the window he won't fall.
   **B** ☐ a clear, cold winter day with snow on the ground.
   **C** ☐ people and events from his past.

**6** When Scrooge sees himself as a young boy, he wishes he had
   **A** ☐ given some money to a boy singing a Christmas carol outside his door.
   **B** ☐ seen his business friends in London.
   **C** ☐ told the ghost about Ali Baba and his adventures.

# Grammar

**2 Choose the correct adverb for the phrases.**

**1** 'You are a dream or a _____ cooked dinner,' Scrooge said to the ghost.

**2** Jacob Marley shook his chain so _____ that Scrooge had to hold onto his seat!

**3** Hundreds of ghosts were flying about in the air talking _____ .

**4** When the second ghost arrived, Scrooge _____ asked why it had come to him.

**3 Use the correct connective. The first is done as an example.**

> ~~as if~~ • because • so ... that • until • when

**0** The ghost sat on the opposite side of the fire ___*as if*___ it sat there every day.

**1** He talked _____ to sit in silence with those dead eyes looking at him would be too horrible.

**2** The ghost's hair and clothes were moving about _____ they were in the air from a hot oven.

**3** I did nothing to make anyone happy _____ I was alive.

**4** Scrooge was _____ frightened _____ he fell on his knees and raised his hands.

**5** They walked along the road _____ a small town appeared.

## PRE-READING ACTIVITY

# Speaking

**4 Before reading Chapter 3, think about the following questions. Discuss in pairs.**

**1** What do you think makes a good party? Good music? Dancing? Good company? Good food?

**2** What do you think makes a good relationship with a girlfriend or boyfriend?

Chapter 3

# Fezziwig's Party

▶ 4 Scrooge and the ghost left the school and were now standing in the streets of a city. Here the shadows of people passed and repassed, on foot or in buses pulled by horses. The normal, busy streets of a real city. Looking into the shop windows, you could see it was Christmas. It was now evening and the lights had been lit.

The ghost stopped at the door of a big building and asked Scrooge if he knew it.

'Know it!' said Scrooge, 'I had my first job here!'

They went in. Sitting at a tall desk was an old man.

'It's Old Fezziwig!' Scrooge cried in great excitement. 'It's that dear man alive again!'

While they watched, Old Fezziwig put down his pen and looked at the clock. It was seven o'clock. He clapped his hands together and laughed loudly. 'Ebenezer! Dick!'

The Scrooge of the past, a little older than when they last saw him, now came in, followed by his friend, Dick.

'Oh that's Dick Wilkins!' Scrooge told the ghost, 'Poor Dick, he was very fond of me you know.'

'Well, my boys,' Fezziwig said, 'No more work tonight. It's

Christmas Eve, Dick! Christmas Ebenezer! Go and close all the windows up as fast as you can!' And he clapped his hands again.

Off went the young Scrooge and Dick. You never saw windows shut up more quickly. They were back almost as soon as they had left, breathing as hard as race horses after a race.

'Well done!' said Fezziwig, jumping down from his desk like a young man. 'Now clear everything away. We need to make room for the dancing!'

Ebenezer and Dick worked so fast that the shop was empty in no time. Everything was put away, the floor was washed, lights were lit and the fire was made. The work room was now the warmest, driest and most comfortable dancing room you could wish for.

The musician arrived with his violin. He climbed up onto Fezziwig's desk and began to practise his music as loudly as if he were fifty musicians.

Then Mrs Fezziwig came in smiling. She was followed by her three daughters, all friendly. Behind them were six young men who hoped to marry the girls, but whose hearts they broke.

Then everyone else arrived. All the people who worked for Old Fezziwig in his business and all the people who helped Mrs Fezziwig in the house. The cook came in with her brother's friend, the milkman. There was a boy from over the road who was never given enough to eat, and the girl from two doors down.

Twenty couples began to dance. They got the dances wrong, starting where they should finish and finishing where they should have started! But it didn't matter, they were having a lovely time.

At eleven o'clock, the party ended. Mr and Mrs Fezziwig stood

by the door, saying 'Merry Christmas' to everyone as they left. Then there was only Ebenezer and Dick left. The two young men lay in their beds at the back of the shop and talked about how kind and generous Fezziwig was until they fell asleep.

All this time, the old Scrooge had been going mad with happiness. He enjoyed everything, remembered everything and became strangely excited by what he saw. Now, he remembered the ghost.

'A small thing,' the ghost said, 'to make these fools so happy.'

'Small!' said Scrooge.

'But he only spent three or four pounds* on them. Why do they love him for such a small amount?'

'It isn't that!' said Scrooge, feeling cross. 'Fezziwig is the man we work for and so he has the power to make us happy or unhappy. He has the power to make our work enjoyable or terrible. It only takes a kind word or look. Small things, but the happiness they give are as if he had spent hundreds of pounds on us!'

He felt the ghost look at him and stopped.

'What's the matter?' asked the ghost.

'Nothing, really,' said Scrooge, then with the ghost still looking at him he said, 'I would like to say a word or two to my clerk. That's all.'

He and the ghost were outside again. Scrooge was a few years older now. His face was beginning to show signs of what he would become. His eyes shone with a growing love of money.

He was not alone. A young girl was standing next to him. She had tears in her eyes and she was speaking. 'When we were young and poor, we made a promise to each other. We said we would work

**pound** unit of money in the UK

hard, and when we had enough money we would marry. But now you don't have room in your heart for me, something else fills your heart.'

'What else fills my heart?'

'A love of gold,' she replied.

'I was a boy,' he said.

'You've changed. I've watched your hopes and dreams disappear. Now you have nothing left but your love of money,' she said.

'Even if I have different dreams now, my feelings for you haven't changed,' he said.

'You know that's not true. I was happy when our hearts were one. I've thought about this for a long time and I understand we must leave each other. You can now be free of me.'

'Have I ever asked to be free of you?' Scrooge said.

'Not with words, no.'

'In what, then?'

'You don't think my love is important any more. There's no room in your life for me,' she said quietly.

'If that's what you say,' he said.

'Even if what I say wasn't true, I don't believe you'd marry a girl like me who has no money. I think you did love me once,' she said, getting ready to leave. 'I hope that for a short time you'll think of what you've lost and be sad. Then, very soon, you'll think of me only as a bad dream and be glad that I am gone.'

'Show me no more!' Scrooge said to the ghost. 'Why do you want me to suffer like this?'

'I have one more thing to show you,' the ghost said.

Now they stood in a small but comfortable room. A mother sat with her daughter who was aged around seventeen. The room was full of children running, shouting, playing. They pulled the shoes from their sister's feet, pulled her hair. But no one seemed to care. In fact, the mother and her daughter were laughing happily.

There was a knock at the door. In came the father of the family, followed by a man carrying presents. The children started shouting with excitement and climbed onto the man, pulling presents out of his arms. The room filled with cries of happiness as the children opened their presents. Then someone saw that the baby had a small toy in her mouth. Everything stopped. Had she eaten any other toy? There were no toys missing, the baby was fine. Everyone started laughing, running and shouting again. At last, the children went upstairs to go to bed and the room was quiet.

The mother sat by the fire and the daughter, who looked so like her mother, sat by her father.

Scrooge's eyes filled with tears as he thought that this young girl might have called him father.

'Belle,' the husband said, turning to his wife. 'I saw an old friend of yours today.'

'Who?' said the wife, 'Oh, don't tell me, I know! It was Scrooge.'

'Yes,' her husband answered. 'I saw him through the window of his office. His old partner, Jacob Marley, is close to death I think and he's completely alone in this world.'

'Ghost,' said Scrooge, 'take me away. I can't watch this!'

'I can't change the past,' said the ghost, and his face seemed to be filled with all the faces of Scrooge's past.

Scrooge began to fight the ghost. He took his night hat and pushed it down over the ghost's head to put out its light. Then he fell into bed and went straight to sleep.

When Scrooge woke again, he didn't need a clock to tell him it was nearly one o'clock again! He thought about the second ghost promised by Marley. Which of the curtains round his bed would *this* ghost open? He felt so frightened, he opened all the curtains himself and lay in bed watching.

Scrooge was not a man of adventure, but he felt ready to see what strange thing might appear in his room.

He was well prepared for something to arrive, but he was not prepared for nothing to appear. He waited, and when the clock rang one and no shape appeared, he started to shake with fear. Five minutes, ten minutes, and still nothing came.

One thing had happened though when the clock rang – his room filled with a bright light. Only light, nothing else. This was more worrying for Scrooge than if his room had filled with twelve ghosts. He couldn't understand what the light was and what it might mean.

At last he began to see that the light was coming from the next room. He got up quietly and walked over to it. As he put his hand on the door, a voice called his name and told him to come in.

It was his own room, he was sure of that, but he hardly recognised it. The walls and ceiling were covered in holly and other plants. Everywhere was so green the room looked like a small wood. There was a huge fire!

The floor was covered with the most delicious food you could imagine. There were turkeys and chickens, meat and puddings, cakes, red apples and fresh oranges, delicious pears and bowls of hot drink.

Sitting on a large chair, looking comfortable and happy, was a huge man. In his hand was a burning light.

'Come in!' he said. 'Come in and know me better, man!'

Scrooge came in with his head low. He was not the same Scrooge as he had been. He didn't want to look into the eyes of this ghost.

'I am the Ghost of Christmas Present,' he said. 'Look at me!'

Hearing this, Scrooge looked at him with respect. He was wearing a large, dark green dress, made pretty with white around the edges. The dress was open at the top and his feet had no shoes or socks on them. On his head was a circle of green holly with pieces of ice hanging down between the leaves. His hair was long and dark. His smiling face was warm and welcoming.

'I don't think you've seen anything like me before, have you?' he said in a friendly voice.

'Never,' said Scrooge.

'But I have many hundreds of brothers. A new one is born every Christmas!' he said.

'That's a big family to feed,' said Scrooge, carefully.

The Ghost of Christmas Present stood.

'Ghost, take me where you want,' said Scrooge. 'Another ghost came and took me on a journey last night, and I learned a lesson which is working now. Tonight, if you have something to teach me, then let me learn from it.'

'Then hold my dress and we will go,' the ghost said.

# Comprehension

**1  Put in order!**

**1**  Ebenezer and Dick help Fezziwig prepare for his party. Put what they do in the correct order.
- [ ] **A**  They cleared everything away to make room for the dancing.
- [ ] **B**  They went to close all the windows up.
- [ ] **C**  They stopped work.
- [ ] **D**  They came back breathing as hard as race horses after a race.
- [ ] **E**  They washed the floor, lit the lights and made the fire.

**2**  What do Belle and Scrooge say to each other? Put their words in the right order.
- [ ] **A**  **Belle:** When we were young and poor, we made a promise to marry each other, now something else fills your heart.
- [ ] **B**  **Belle:** Not in words, no. Goodbye Ebenezer. I hope that you'll think of what you've lost and be sad.
- [ ] **C**  **Scrooge:** My feelings for you haven't changed. I've never asked to be free of you.
- [ ] **D**  **Scrooge:** I was a boy.
- [ ] **E**  **Belle:** As we've grown older, I've watched your hopes and dreams disappear. Now you only have your love of money.

**3**  What happens when the church clock tells Scrooge it's one o'clock again? Put the events in the correct order.
- [ ] **A**  He saw that the light was coming from the next room.
- [ ] **B**  Scrooge felt so frightened, he opened all the curtains and lay in bed watching.
- [ ] **C**  As he put his hand on the door, a voice called his name and told him to come in.
- [ ] **D**  His room filled with a bright light, but nothing else.
- [ ] **E**  A huge, happy man, was sitting on a large, comfortable chair in Scrooge's sitting room.

# Vocabulary

**2** Which adjectives and adjectival phrases best describe each Scrooge? (There are four for each section.)

> ashamed • cold • full of energy • hard hearted •
> hard working • horrible • keen • mad with happiness •
> quick • selfish • sorry • upset

| Scrooge when he works with Fezziwig | Scrooge when Belle leaves him | Scrooge with the Ghost of Christmas Past |
|---|---|---|
| | | |
| | | |
| | | |
| | | |

## PRE-READING ACTIVITY

▶ 5 **3** Read these phrases, then, as you listen to the first part of Chapter 4, tick each one that you hear.

- ☐ no longer night
- ☐ standing on the dirty streets
- ☐ clearing snow from the streets
- ☐ some were at the front of their houses
- ☐ pushing great mountains of snow off
- ☐ hit the ground like little snow storms
- ☐ throwing snowballs at each other
- ☐ laughed just as loudly if the snowball missed
- ☐ the shops were already shut
- ☐ they would make your mouth water

Chapter 4

# The Ghost of Christmas Present

▶ 5 As soon as Scrooge touched the ghost's dark green dress, the room disappeared. The holly, the food, the fruit and drink and the fire were gone and it was no longer night.

Scrooge and the Ghost of Christmas Present were standing in the city streets. It was a cold Christmas morning. The people were clearing snow from the streets in front of their houses. Some were up on the roofs, pushing great mountains of snow off onto the street below. Boys stood watching and laughing when the snow fell off the roofs and hit the ground like little snow storms.

The fronts of the houses were black and the windows dirty, while the snow on the roofs was clean and white. The sky was dark too. Despite this, everyone looked happy and called out to one another from the roofs. Many of them were playing with the snow, throwing snowballs at each other. Everyone laughed when a snowball hit someone, but they laughed just as loudly if the snowball missed!

The shops were beginning to shut, but there were a lot of people about trying to buy the last things they needed. There were mountains of nuts and large Spanish onions, pears and apples, bright oranges and lemons and grapes that looked so sweet they would make your mouth water! ■

The shops selling chickens, turkeys and geese* were almost closed. In other shops, assistants were running around, wrapping things up and packing them in bags and baskets. The food all looked as though it was asking to be put into a paper bag and taken home.

The air was filled with the smell of tea and coffee, the dried fruit looked of the highest quality, and ingredients from countries far away were the best that you could buy. There was fruit covered in sugar that looked so sweet it might make you feel ill and other pretty sweets from France in lovely boxes.

The customers were all in such a hurry on this happy, busy day, that they were trying to get into the shops at the same time. They rushed about, pushing into each other. Some were moving about so fast that they left what they had bought in the shop and had to go back for it! But no one got cross during all these hundreds of little mistakes.

Soon the church bells began to ring, calling everyone to church. The streets filled with people wearing their best clothes and the happiest faces.

At the same time, from the back streets, poor people appeared carrying a goose or a turkey to the baker's, who allowed them to use his hot oven to cook their Christmas dinner because they didn't have anywhere to cook them at home. These people seemed to be of great interest to the ghost. He stood at the door of the baker's with Scrooge. As these poor people passed, he lifted the tops off the saucepans and shook in some magic from his burning light.

Once or twice there were angry words when people carrying their dinners walked into each other. He put some drops of magic on to

**goose** (plural geese) large water bird, bigger than a duck. Often white.

them and they forgot to be cross. It would be a shame to be cross on Christmas Day!

After a time, the church bells stopped ringing, and the baker's shops shut, but you could still smell the dinners cooking. The heat from the ovens made the snow turn to water.

'Do you give your magic to any kind of dinner on Christmas Day?' Scrooge asked the ghost.

'To any dinner that is kindly given, but I give most of my magic to the poor.'

'Why?'

'Because they need it most,' he answered.

'But they say you want to close all baker's shops on Sundays so that no one has to work on God's special day. These poor people don't have ovens at home,' Scrooge said, 'they need the baker's to cook their meals .'

'*I want? Not I!*' cried the ghost. 'There are many people on this earth who think they know what I want. They do a lot of bad things and then they tell everyone they're doing what I want. They know nothing about me and they are no friends of mine. Remember that, and do *not* blame me for the terrible things they do.'

Scrooge promised he would remember what the ghost said.

Scrooge held onto the ghost and they walked away from the centre of the city towards Camden Town. Perhaps it was the great kindness of the ghost towards poor people that made him take Scrooge to his clerk's house.

When they got to Bob Cratchit's door, the ghost stopped and dropped some magic on this little house which only had four rooms.

Inside, Mrs Cratchit was wearing an old dress, made as pretty as possible with coloured silks.

She and her daughter Belinda made the table look nice, while her oldest son, Peter, looked after the potatoes. The two younger children came screaming into the house saying they'd been to the baker's and could smell their goose cooking. They ran around getting more and more excited as they thought about the delicious goose flavoured with onion and herbs.

Peter blew on the fire to make the potatoes boil. The water heated up and soon the potatoes were knocking on the top of the saucepan as if they wanted to be let out.

'Where's your father?' said Mrs Cratchit, 'And Tiny Tim! And Martha is late too!'

'Here's Martha,' said a girl at the door.

'Here's Martha, Mother,' cried the two younger Cratchits, 'Hooray! There is *such* a goose Martha!'

Mrs Cratchit left what she was doing and went to hold and kiss her eldest daughter.

'We had so many dresses and shirts to finish last night,' the girl said, 'and we had to make everything tidy this morning, Mother!'

'Oh, don't worry,' her mother said, 'come and warm yourself by the fire.'

But Martha didn't have time to sit, before the two younger Cratchits told her to hide because father was arriving with Tiny Tim on his shoulders!

Into the house came Bob Cratchit. Tiny Tim had been very ill as a child and couldn't walk very well.

'Where's Martha?' asked Bob.

'Not coming,' said Mrs Cratchit.

When he heard that, Bob looked so sad that Martha ran straight out of the cupboard where she was hiding and put her arms round him.

The two younger Cratchits took Tiny Tim to the wash house behind their home. This is where the Christmas pudding was, in a huge pot that Mrs Cratchit normally used to boil the sheets and shirts to wash them. Today, the pudding was boiling there instead, wrapped in a clean cloth.

'How was Tiny Tim?' Mrs Cratchit asked her husband.

'He says such deep things,' answered Bob, 'he thinks about God a lot. He told me he hoped the people would see him in church and remember that God always tried to help children like him.'

Bob was sad when he said this. It seemed as if he would cry when he said to his wife how strong Tim was growing. It was obvious that the opposite was true.

Tiny Tim came back into the house with his brother and sister. Bob put some tea, lemons and water in a pot and put it on the fire next to the potatoes. Then Bob told Peter and the two youngest to go to the baker's to get the goose, which was certainly ready by now.

They came back with the goose, holding it as high as if it was the king of all the birds. Belinda made the apple sauce, Peter prepared the potatoes. The two young Cratchits got chairs for everyone, including a little seat for Tiny Tim. Then they sat at the table and put spoons in their mouths. This was to stop themselves screaming with excitement about the goose, with the onions and herbs.

When everyone was at the table, Mrs Cratchit took the knife and cut the bird. When they had finished their dinner they all said it was the best goose they had ever eaten!

The children cleared the table and Mrs Cratchit went out to the wash house to get the pudding. She didn't want anyone with her. She was worried it might not be cooked, or that it might break into pieces when she took it out of its cloth. Or perhaps someone had come to the back of the house and stolen it when they were eating the goose! The two younger Cratchits got very cross when they thought that someone might have stolen the pudding!

But none of them needed to worry. Mrs Cratchit soon arrived with the pudding made pretty with a piece of holly on the top.

Bob said it was the best pudding his wife had ever made. Everyone said something good about the pudding, but none of them said it was a little small for eight of them to eat. That never entered into their thoughts.

When the meal was ended, they sat in a half circle around the fire and had the hot tea and lemon.

'Merry Christmas to us all, my dears!' he said. 'God bless us!'

'God bless us!' everyone shouted.

'God bless us everyone,' said Tiny Tim, in his little voice.

He sat very close to his father and sang a lovely song. Bob held his little hand as if he was worried that the child might be taken from him. He wanted him never to leave.

'Ghost,' said Scrooge, with an interest in the child that he'd never felt before. 'Tell me if Tiny Tim will die.'

'I see an empty seat,' the ghost replied. 'An empty seat in the corner next to the fire, with a walking stick lying next to it.'

'Tell me that isn't true!'

'If these shadows do not change,' the ghost continued, 'then this child will die.'

'No, no,' said Scrooge. 'Oh no, kind ghost! Tell me he won't die!'

'If these shadows stay the same, if nothing changes in the future, then none of us will see him next Christmas. But that shouldn't be anything to worry you. If he wants to die then he should die quickly. If he was dead we wouldn't have so many people to feed.'

Scrooge felt deep shame to hear the ghost repeat his own words back to him.

'Will you decide who lives and who dies?' asked the ghost. 'It may be that in God's eyes you are worth less than this child and millions like him.'

Scrooge looked at the ground and his eyes filled with tears.

They left the Cratchits and the ghost took Scrooge to the homes of other poor people, where families sang Christmas Carols together. He took Scrooge to a ship on the sea, where the sailors thought about their loved ones at home and were a little kinder to each other because it was Christmas Day.

Scrooge was standing on the ship, listening to the wind, thinking about how strange it was to be travelling over the deep, dark ocean, when he suddenly heard someone laughing happily. He recognised that laugh! It was his nephew!

Scrooge was even more surprised to be standing in a clean, dry, bright room that was his nephew's. The ghost was standing by his side, looking at Scrooge's nephew and smiling.

'Ha ha,' laughed Scrooge's nephew, 'Ha, ha, ha!'

# Comprehension

**1** **Use the words to help you write the questions for these answers! The first one is done to help you.**

**0** *What were people doing up on the roofs?*

people | do | roofs
*They were pushing snow off and throwing snowballs at each other.*

**1** _____

streets | fill | happy people | wear | best clothes
*Because the church bells were ringing, calling everyone to church.*

**2** _____

Ghost | Christmas | Present | shake | magic | people
*So that they would forget to be cross with each other.*

**3** _____

Ghost | Christmas | Present | cross
*Because he said people did a lot of bad things and then told everyone it was what he wanted!*

**4** _____

cook | pot | Mrs Cratchit | normally | wash | clothes
*The Christmas Pudding, wrapped in a clean cloth.*

**5** _____

Ghost | say | happen | Tiny Tim
*He said that if nothing changed in the future, then Tiny Tim would die.*

**6** _____

Scrooge | ashamed
*Because the Ghost repeated his cruel words about poor people.*

**7** _____

Scrooge's nephew | do
*He was standing in a clean, dry, bright room laughing.*

# Grammar

**2 Make these sentences simpler using 'each other'.**

**1** Some boys were throwing snow balls at other boys and the other boys were throwing some back.

_____

**2** Everyone was in such a hurry. One person pushed into three people, then those people pushed into other people!

_____

**3** When the Cratchits had finished, Bob looked at Mrs Cratchit and the children, and she and the children looked at him, and they all said it was the best goose ever.

_____

**3 Put these sentences into reported speech. The first is done to help you.**

**0** 'Those poor people don't have ovens at home,' said Scrooge.
_Scrooge said (those) poor people didn't have ovens at home._

**1** 'Where's your father and where's Martha?' Mrs Cratchit asked.

_____

**2** 'We had to make everything tidy this morning, Mother,' Martha said.

_____

**3** 'I hope everyone will remember that God helps children like me,' said Tiny Tim.

_____

## PRE-READING ACTIVITY

▶ 6 **4 Try to answer these questions, then listen to the first part of Chapter 5 and see if you were right.**

**1** Why were Scrooge's nephew, his wife and their friends all laughing loudly?

_____

**2** What does Scrooge's nephew think of Scrooge and his money?

_____

Chapter 5

# The Ghost of Christmas Yet to Come

▶ 6 Scrooge's nephew was standing in the middle of his room and he was laughing. He had the best laugh I've ever heard. If you happen to know anyone with a better laugh, I would like to meet them!

You can catch all kinds of illnesses from people and when someone is sad, it is quite natural for you to feel sad with them. I am glad, then, that you can also 'catch' laughter from people just as easily as you can catch illnesses and sadness. This makes our world a much fairer place.

When Scrooge's nephew laughed in this way, holding his sides, moving his head about in the strangest way, his wife also laughed. Their friends, who were celebrating Christmas with them, were laughing just as loudly.

'Ha, ha! Ha, ha, ha, ha, ha!'

What were they laughing about?

'He said that Christmas was a humbug. It's true!' cried Scrooge's nephew. 'And he believed it, too!'

'Well, it's not right, Fred,' said Scrooge's wife, crossly.

'He's certainly a strange old man,' said Scrooge's nephew, 'that's the truth, and he's not as nice as he could be. However, he's only making his life worse for himself and I have nothing to say against him.'

'I'm sure he is very rich, Fred,' said his wife. 'At least you always tell me so.'

'His money is no use to him and he doesn't help anyone else with it. He can't even enjoy the thought – ha, ha, ha! – that he will ever help us out with his money!'

'Well, he makes me cross,' she answered. Her sisters and all the other ladies in the room agreed.

'Oh, I feel sorry for him,' said Scrooge's nephew, 'I couldn't be angry with him if I tried. Who suffers when he is so cross all the time? Only he does. He decides he doesn't like us and won't come to dinner with us – what's the problem with that? He doesn't miss much!'

'He misses a very good dinner!' said his wife. Everybody else said the same, and you should probably believe them because they had just finished their dinner. The pudding was on the table and they were standing round the fire and the room was lit by lamps.

'I was only going to say that the result of him not liking us and not coming to celebrate Christmas with us, is that he misses having a nice time. It would do him good to enjoy himself. I am sure he would find us nicer to be with than his own thoughts. Every Christmas I will go to his terrible old offices and I will ask him to have dinner with us. He will probably get angry about Christmas every year, but if I go in smiling year after year, then he might think about leaving his poor clerk fifty pounds. I would be happy with that. I think he was beginning to listen to me when I went to see him yesterday.'

His wife and friends stopped laughing about Scrooge and laughed at his nephew next! They found it hard to believe that Scrooge would listen to his nephew even for half a minute.

After the pudding they played some music. They played a song that Scrooge's sister had liked when she was young.

When he heard this music, Scrooge thought about all the things he had seen that night. He thought that if he could have listened to it often, years ago, he might have lived a happier life.

When they had had enough of music, Scrooge's nephew, his wife and their friends played some games. Scrooge and the ghost were standing just behind Fred's wife. Scrooge shouted out all the answers to the questions. He often got the answers right too.

The ghost was very pleased to see Scrooge so happy. Scrooge was enjoying himself so much that he asked the ghost if they could stay until the guests went, but the ghost said this was not possible.

'They're starting a new game, Ghost,' said Scrooge, 'at least let me listen to this.'

It was a game called Yes and No. Scrooge's nephew had to think of something and the others had to find out what by asking him questions. Fred could only answer yes or no. The others threw many questions at him. In this way, they discovered that he was thinking of an animal. This animal was alive and was an unfriendly animal. It lived in London, but nobody looked after it, it didn't live in a zoo but walked about the streets. It wasn't a horse, a cow or a tiger and it wasn't a dog, a pig, a cat or a bear. Every time they asked him a question, Scrooge's nephew started laughing! In fact, He found it so funny that he had to get up from the sofa and walk round the room.

At last, one of his wife's sisters cried out, 'I have found it out! I know what it is, Fred! I know what it is!'

'What is it?' cried Fred.

'It's your Uncle Scrooge.'

She was right, of course.

'Well, he has given us a lot to laugh about,' said Fred, 'so let's all wish Uncle Scrooge a Merry Christmas.'

They raised their glasses, 'To Uncle Scrooge,' they said.

'A Merry Christmas and a Happy New Year to the old man!'

When he heard this, Scrooge became so happy and excited that he would have returned the wish to his nephew and his family and friends. But the ghost gave him no time. As Fred said these words, the room disappeared. Scrooge and the ghost were travelling again.

They saw a lot of things and visited many homes. The ghost gave his blessing to everyone they saw. If a person was ill, the ghost stood next to them and they were happy, if they were poor, they felt rich.

It was a long night. The ghost was starting to look old.

'Do all ghosts have such a short life as you?' Scrooge asked.

'My life in this world is very short, it ends tonight.'

Scrooge was surprised. Then he saw something hiding under the ghost's clothes.

'Forgive me for asking,' he said, 'but what is hiding there?'

A boy and a girl appeared in front of the ghost. They were yellow, thin and poor, and terrible to look at. They didn't look like children should look. They should have had the faces of angels, instead they looked like devils.

They looked so disgusting that Scrooge took a step back.

'Are they your children, Ghost?'

'No, they are the children of man.'

'The boy is for everyone who chooses not to see, the girl is for everyone who does not have enough,' the ghost continued.

'Isn't there anyone who will look after them?'

'Are there no prisons?' said the ghost, using Scrooge's own words again, 'are there no poorhouses?'

The clock bell rang twelve.

Scrooge looked for the ghost, but he and the two children had disappeared. As the bell rang for the twelfth time, he remembered what Jacob Marley had said about the third ghost. He looked up. Coming towards him, like fog moving across the ground, was the third ghost. It had a long, dark coat. Its head was completely covered with a hood* so large that you could not see its face, you couldn't even see the light from its eyes.

Slowly, silently the third and most terrifying ghost came towards Scrooge. While the other ghosts had given out light, this one seemed to make everything around it darker and more serious. As it got closer, it reached out a hand and stopped.

'Are you the Ghost of Christmas Yet to Come?' asked Scrooge.

The ghost didn't move and it didn't answer.

'Have you come to show me things that will happen in the future?'

The ghost moved his head as if to say yes.

Although he was quite used to ghosts by now, this one made Scrooge more frightened that he had ever been in his life. It made him ill to think of those eyes he couldn't see, watching him from under that black hood.

'Ghost of the future,' said Scrooge. 'I am more frightened of you than of the other ghosts I have seen tonight, but I know you are here

hood part of a coat that you can pull up to cover your head

to do me good. Show me what you want to show so that I can learn.'

The ghost moved away along the ground and Scrooge followed it into the City of London, where bankers and businessmen work. They heard two large rich men talking.

'When did he die?' one of them asked.

'Last night, I think.'

'What has he done with his money?'

'I don't know. He hasn't left it to *me*,' his friend said with a laugh.

Others joined them. 'At least one of us should go to the church when he is buried,' one of them said.

'Well, I'm only going if we are given lunch,' the large man said. They all laughed at that.

Scrooge knew all of these men but he didn't understand what they were talking about. The ghost didn't say a word, but moved silently into another street. Here was another conversation.

'How are you?' said one man to another.

'Well. How are you?' answered his friend. 'Did you hear he's died?'

'Yes. Cold, isn't it?'

'It's what you would expect at Christmas!'

They raised their hats and left.

Scrooge was surprised that the ghost was showing him all these unimportant conversations, but he thought they probably had some hidden meaning.

This time, they went to the darkest and most miserable part of London where only the worst people went. Scrooge had never been here before, but he followed the ghost to a shop whose windows were so dirty you could hardly see inside.

# Comprehension

**1** **What is the right answer, A, B, or C?**

**1** The writer says the world is a fairer place because
- **A** ☐ he would like to meet someone with a better laugh than Fred.
- **B** ☐ when someone is sad it is natural for you to feel sad with them.
- **C** ☐ although we can catch diseases and sadness from people, you can catch laughter just as easily.

**2** Fred says he will visit his uncle every year at Christmas
- **A** ☐ so he might become kinder and leave Bob a bit of money when he dies.
- **B** ☐ because he will enjoy making his uncle cross.
- **C** ☐ because he wants to make those terrible old offices nicer at Christmas.

**3** Fred said they should wish Uncle Scrooge a Merry Christmas because
- **A** ☐ his wife's sister guessed the answer correctly.
- **B** ☐ he'd given them plenty to laugh about.
- **C** ☐ Christmas is a time when everyone is nicer to each other.

**4** Scrooge was enjoying himself so much that he asked the ghost
- **A** ☐ to let him go to another party.
- **B** ☐ to let him stay a little longer.
- **C** ☐ to let Fred know what a good party it was.

**5** What was hiding under the ghost's clothes?
- **A** ☐ Two children that Scrooge said should be in the poorhouse.
- **B** ☐ Two children that the ghost was trying to help.
- **C** ☐ Two children who were another lesson for Scrooge.

**6** What does the third ghost look like?
- **A** ☐ He had a serious, terrifying face.
- **B** ☐ He had a long dark coat and a hood that covered his face.
- **C** ☐ Scrooge was so frightened, that he couldn't see the ghost's eyes.

# Vocabulary

**2** **Write a definition or synonym of these words. Then write a sentence using each one. The first is done to help you.**

**0** **illness**    _period of time when you are ill_
_He had a serious illness when he was a child, and now he can't_
_walk very well._

**1** **suffer** _____
_____
_____

**2** **fair** _____
_____
_____

**3** **agree** _____
_____
_____

**4** **raise** _____
_____
_____

## PRE-READING ACTIVITY

**3a** **Read the start of Chapter 6. What do you think is happening?**

Scrooge and the ghost went into the shop. It was filled with bits of old metal, dirty cloths and bones, all separated into groups. Behind a dirty curtain of old cloth, there sat an old man. At that moment, a cleaning woman came in carrying a big cloth tied at the top. Immediately behind her were another woman and a man in an old black suit.
'Let me be first, Old Joe,' said the cleaning woman.

**3b** **After reading, were you right? Did anything surprise or shock you?**

Chapter 6

# The End of It

▶ 7 Scrooge and the ghost went into the shop. It was filled with bits of old metal, dirty cloths and bones, all separated into groups. Behind a dirty curtain of old cloth, there sat an old man. At that moment, a cleaning woman came in carrying a big cloth tied at the top. Immediately behind her were another woman and a man in an old black suit.

'Let me be first, Old Joe,' said the cleaning woman, 'after me you can see what the woman who washes the clothes has brought, and after her, see what the man who got his body ready after he died has brought you!'

'Come in! Come in!' said Old Joe.

They went behind the dirty cloth to the back of the shop.

'There's no need for any of us to feel bad about this,' the first woman said, 'he won't know we taken these few things. If he had wanted to keep them after he died, then he should have been nicer when he was alive. As it was, he took his last breath all alone, so there was no one there to look after his things.'

'Very true,' the other woman said.

First the man took out of his pockets what he had taken from the dead man. There wasn't a lot, a pencil case and two or three pieces of inexpensive jewellery. Old Joe wrote what he would pay for each piece on the wall, then added it up. He did the same for the second

woman. She had two silver teaspoons, sheets and towels, a pair of trousers and some boots.

Finally, the first woman opened up her cloth.

'What is this?' cried Old Joe. 'Bed curtains!'

The woman looked at him and laughed.

'Did you take the curtains off his bed, rings and all, while he was lying there dead?' Old Joe asked.

'Be careful of the blankets!' she continued.

'His blankets?'

'Of course. He can't get any colder without them, can he?'

'What did he die of? We won't catch anything from him, will we?' Old Joe asked.

'Don't worry about that,' she said, 'I wouldn't have taken them if he did. Here's his best shirt. I didn't want them to waste that.'

Then they all began to laugh.

Scrooge looked at the four as if they were devils arguing about how much they would sell the body for.

'This was his end,' when Old Joe had handed out the money. 'He frightened everyone away from him when he was alive, so that we could make a bit of money from him when he was dead!'

'Ghost!' said Scrooge shaking from head to foot. 'I see the lesson you want to teach me. This dead man could have been me.'

Suddenly, they were standing by a bed. On it, covered with a sheet, was something that Scrooge did not want to see. The ghost pointed to the head of the body lying on the bed.

'Ghost, this is a terrible place. I won't forget this lesson when we leave. Let us go!'

Still the ghost pointed at the head.

'I don't have the power to look at that head,' said Scrooge. 'Let me see if there is anyone in this city that feels anything about this man's death.'

The ghost took him to a small house where a young man was talking with his wife.

'Now that he's dead, we'll have a bit more time to find the money to pay back what we borrowed,' the man said.

'Then, God forgive me Arthur, but I'm glad he died,' the young woman replied.

'I'm sorry to say it too, but we may sleep in our beds with lighter hearts tonight, Caroline.'

'Ghost, show me a house where people *are* sad because someone has died.'


Scrooge found himself in Bob Cratchit's house. Mrs Cratchit and the children were all quiet in the room when Bob came in. His tea was ready on the fire and they all ran to get it ready for him. Bob sat by the fire and the two younger Cratchits each sat on a knee, resting their heads on his cheeks.

'It's very green, where he is going,' Bob said, 'but we will go there often, I told him I would go every Sunday.' Then he started to cry, 'My little, little child!' cried Bob, 'My little child!'

He left the room and went upstairs where Tiny Tim's body was lying. He sat in a chair next to his son and when he felt calmer, he got up, kissed Tiny Tim's forehead and went back downstairs.

The Cratchits sat round the fire and talked. Bob told them he had seen Scrooge's nephew in the street.

'He said he was very sorry to hear about Tiny Tim, and very sorry for my good wife!

'He's a good man,' Mrs Cratchit said.

'He might even find Peter a job,' said Bob.

'Then you'll meet a girl and leave us, Peter!' said one of the girls.

'Well, that will happen sooner or later,' agreed Bob, 'but however and whenever we leave each other, I am sure we will never forget Tiny Tim.'

'Never Father!' they all cried.

'And when we remember how patient and gentle he was, even though he was only a little, little child, we will not get cross with each other and forget about him.'

'No, never, Father,' they all cried again.

'I am very happy,' said Bob, 'I am very happy.'

'Ghost,' said Scrooge, 'I would like to know who that dead man was that we saw lying on his bed.'

The ghost took him through the city, past his old office, where now someone else sat at a desk, and to a church. The dead were buried in the small area around the church. The ghost took Scrooge towards a stone with a name on it to show who was buried there.

'Before I get near that stone,' Scrooge said, 'answer me one question. Are these the shadows of things that will be, or are they the shadows of the things that *might* be?'

The ghost said nothing. He pointed at the stone.

'Tell me I can change the future!'

The ghost stood silently pointing at the stone.

So, Scrooge walked towards it with legs that shook and on it he read the words, Ebenezer Scrooge.

'No, ghost! Oh, no, no!'

Scrooge held the ghost's coat tight, but still the ghost pointed.

'I am not the man I was,' said Scrooge. 'Why do you show me these things if there is no hope for me!'

The ghost's hand began to shake.

'Good ghost,' he said, throwing himself at the ghost's feet, 'I will change my life and change the shadows that you have shown me! I will celebrate Christmas and keep it all year. I will learn the lessons that the three ghosts have shown me. Tell me I can change the writing on this stone.'

Scrooge found himself alone. He was back in bed. The bed was his own bed and he was still alive! Best and happiest of all, now he would be able to do everything differently.

'I will live in the past, the present and the future!' Scrooge repeated, and he got out of bed and ran round his room. 'O Jacob Marley, thank you. I go down on my knees to thank you, Jacob!'

He went back to his bed and took one of the curtains in his arms. 'My curtains are still here! They are here, I am here, the shadows of the future have been changed!'

'I don't know what to do!' he said, dancing round the room, 'I am as happy as an angel, as merry as a school boy! A Merry Christmas to everybody! A Happy New Year to all the world!'

He danced out of the bedroom and into the sitting room.

'There's the door where the ghost of Jacob Marley came in! There's the corner where the Ghost of Christmas Present sat! There's

the window where I saw all those ghosts flying about in the air! It's all right, it's all true, it all happened! Ha, ha ha!'

Although he had not laughed for years, Scrooge had a wonderful laugh.

'I don't know what day of the month it is!' continued Scrooge, 'I don't know how long I was with the ghosts!'

At that moment, all the church bells began to ring louder than he had ever heard. He ran to the window and opened it. The fog had gone and the day was bright and clear. Oh, wonderful day!

'What's today?' cried Scrooge to a boy below.

'Eh?' he answered.

'What's today, young man?' he asked again.

Today?' he said, 'It's Christmas Day!'

'It's Christmas Day,' Scrooge said to himself, 'I haven't missed it!' Then he called down to the boy again.

'Have they sold that big turkey round the corner?'

'What, the one that's as big as me? That's still for sale,' the boy replied.

'What a lovely boy,' said Scrooge, 'it's a pleasure to talk to him! Then go and buy it for me. Come back with the man and I will give you some money. If you are back with the man in under five minutes, I'll give you double!'

The boy ran off as fast as his legs would take him.

'I'll send it to Bob Cratchit's,' Scrooge said to himself. 'He won't know who has sent it. That turkey is twice the size of Tiny Tim!'

Scrooge went downstairs to wait for the turkey. When the boy came back, Scrooge wrote down the Cratchit's address with a shaking hand.

He laughed as he paid the man for the turkey, he laughed as he paid the boy. He went back upstairs and laughed until he cried. Then he put on his best clothes and went out into the streets.

The streets were as busy and full of people as he had seen with the Ghost of Christmas Present. He walked with his hands behind his back and with such a smile on his face that three or four people said, 'Good morning, Sir. A Merry Christmas to you!'

For a long time after that, Scrooge said that was the nicest thing he'd ever heard.

Then he saw the man who had come into his office the day before, asking for money to help the poor. Scrooge thought the man probably wouldn't want to speak to him, but he walked quickly to meet him.

'My dear sir,' said Scrooge, 'A Merry Christmas to you! I hope you did well yesterday, it was very kind of you, sir!'

'Mr Scrooge?'

'Yes, that's my name, and I don't think it's a name you'll want to hear, but please allow me to ask for your forgiveness. I would like to help you. Will you accept...' and he spoke quietly in the man's ear.

'God bless you, Sir!' the man said, 'Are you serious?'

'I am,' Scrooge replied, shaking hands with him.

'I don't know what to say to such a large amount!'

'Don't say anything, please. Come and see me tomorrow.'

'I will!' the man said.


Scrooge spent several hours walking through the streets. He watched people hurrying about, spoke to children, asked homeless men and

women about their lives. He looked in through the windows of kitchens and sitting rooms, and found that everything he saw made him happy.

In the afternoon, he walked to his nephew's house. Scrooge's nephew and his wife were in the dining room, preparing for their Christmas dinner.

'Fred!' said Scrooge, as he came round the door. Fred's wife nearly fell off her chair in surprise when she saw who it was.

'Why bless me! Who is that?' said Fred, who had his back to the door.

'It is I, your Uncle Scrooge. I have come to have dinner with you, if you still want me?'

Still want him! It's a surprise that Scrooge's arm didn't come off when Fred shook his hand. After five minutes, it was as if he'd always been there. All the friends and family arrived. The party was exactly as he had seen it with the ghost, only this time he was there too!

Next morning, he arrived at the office early. Bob was nearly twenty minutes late!

'I am very sorry, Sir,' Bob said.

'I should think you are sorry,' said Scrooge, trying to use his old voice, 'and so,' then he smiled, 'from today, I will pay you twice as much and look after you and your family. A Merry Christmas, Bob!'

Scrooge did it all and a lot more. He was like a second father to Tiny Tim, who did not die. He became a good man and a good friend. Everyone said he knew how to celebrate Christmas! And so, as Tiny Tim said, God bless us every one!

# Comprehension

**1** **Answer the following questions.**

**1** Why have the two women and the man in the black suit gone to Old Joe's shop?

_____

**2** Where does the ghost take Scrooge after they leave Old Joe's shop, and why?

_____

**3** How did Arthur and Caroline feel about the death of the man?

_____

**4** The ghost takes Scrooge to visit the Cratchits – what has happened?

_____

**5** How does Scrooge find out who the dead man was?

_____

**6** What does Scrooge promise the ghost that he will do from now on?

_____

# Writing

**2** **Write a short description of what Scrooge does and how he is feeling when he wakes up on Christmas morning.**

_____

_____

_____

_____

_____

# Grammar

**3** **Put the verbs into the correct form and tense.**

Scrooge **1** _____ (find) himself alone. He **2** _____ (be) back in bed. The bed was his own bed and he was still alive! Best and happiest of all, now he **3** _____ (be able) to do everything differently.

'I **4** _____ (live) in the past, the present and the future!' Scrooge **5** _____ (repeat), and he got out of bed and ran round his room. 'O Jacob Marley, thank you. I **6** _____ (go) down on my knees to thank you, Jacob!'

He went back to his bed and **7** _____ (take) one of the curtains in his arms. 'My curtains **8** _____ (be) still here! I **9** _____ (be) here, the shadows of the future **10** _____ (be changed)!'

# Speaking

**4** **Think about these questions, then discuss your answers in pairs.**

| Question | Notes |
|---|---|
| **1** What are the biggest lessons that Scrooge has learned from the ghosts? | |
| **2** How has his relationship changed with his clerk and the Cratchit family during this story? | |
| **3** How has Scrooge's relationship with money changed during this story? | |
| **4** How has Scrooge's relationship changed with his nephew? | |
| **5** Find five adjectives to describe the 'new' Scrooge. | |
| **6** Do you think Scrooge has changed or will he go back to being the same old Scrooge of before? | |

# Charles Dickens

A *Christmas Carol* was on sale from December 1843, just in time for Christmas that year. All copies sold in a few days! It is still one of Charles Dickens' most popular stories, 170 years later.

Charles Dickens in 1842, the year before the publication of *A Christmas Carol*.

Historic house in Portsmouth, Hampshire where Charles Dickens was born.

## Family Life

Charles Dickens always knew he was different, even when he was a boy. His father worked in the south of England. The father and his wife, Elizabeth Barrow, had eight children, although two of them died when they were very young. Charles had an older sister, Fanny, born two years before him in 1870. If you remember, when Scrooge visits his old school with the Ghost of Christmas Past, Scrooge's *younger* sister Fan comes to take him home.

## Books and Theatre

For the first nine years of his life, Charles lived happily with his family in a town called Chatham on the river Thames, about thirty miles east of the city of London. He was often ill as a child, but he said that being ill had given him a big advantage – it made him love reading and learning. His father had a small collection of books which Charles read again and again. Of course, it wasn't long before he was writing his own stories.

The young Charles loved telling stories and singing songs, and when his parents had guests over for dinner, he would stand on a chair and entertain them. When he was older he felt embarrassed that these adults had had to sit and watch him! A cousin of his took him to the theatre when he was only six and he loved that too.

## Into Prison

This happy time ended when Charles was nine years old. His father started to have financial problems. The family left Chatham and moved into the poor district of Camden, in North London. This is where the Cratchits live. Worst of all for Charles, he had to leave school. At first he hated London, but he was helped by a family member and borrowed books from other friends. Then his father's money problems got so bad he was sent to a famously terrible prison called Marshalsea! Charles often visited his father during this time.

Then the family sold the collection of books that Charles had loved so much. Still only ten years old, he was sent to work full time. He

Marshalsea.

later told a friend that these experiences as a child were very painful. 'I couldn't understand why no one thought I might be unhappy about going out to work,' he said. 'I loved learning, I was quick and keen, and wanted to go to school. Instead my parents seemed happy that I was bringing a bit of money into the house.'

## From Bad Things...

These early experiences had a big effect on the young writer. He remembered everything, the way of life, the people he met, and then, when he was older, he wrote about it all!
When you know this, you can see why Dickens wrote so much about poor people and why he thought they should be helped. He wants rich people, like Scrooge, to understand that poor people have difficult and sometimes horrible lives.

# England in the 1800s

## A Time of Change

**Charles Dickens used some of the people and places from his childhood in this story, but during the 1830s and 40s many things were changing in England and this is what made Dickens write *A Christmas Carol.***

## Leaving the country

During the early 1800s, for many reasons, people started leaving the country, where they had worked on farms. They were moving to towns and cities to find work. Life was often bad here, houses were small and dark, many people lived together in one or two rooms, there was often no safe drinking water and so on. These people found themselves living next to hundreds of thousands of strangers. People stopped celebrating Christmas because they had lost their old way of life. Dickens thought people needed celebrations to feel happy, which for him was as important as having enough to eat. With *A Christmas Carol* he helped to remind people what a good Christmas should be.

London ironworks.

What did people stop doing when they moved to the cities?
_____

How did poor people live in these new cities?
_____

What did Dickens think was as important as having enough to eat?
_____

The streets of London.

## The Power of A Christmas Carol

This little book, with its story of hope and a fairer world, started to change things from the day it went on sale. After reading it, a number of rich people 'did a Scrooge' and gave money to the poor. People celebrated Christmas as their parents and grandparents had done. Dickens did help to change the idea of all poor people being lazy criminals. Many years later, during the 1910s, people in the UK started to get money if they were out of work. This developed into the modern 'welfare state'. Here, everyone pays part of the money they earn, then if they are ill or lose their job, they will be given some money to live on.

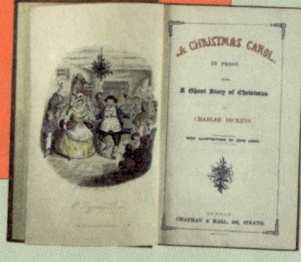
A *Christmas Carol*, first edition.

## The New Poor Law

The second, and more serious problem was the New Poor Law of 1834 – laws are rules which tell people what they can and can't do. Before 1834, each village or town had to give money to the poor. The New Poor Law said help would now only be given in the terrible poorhouses, also known as workhouses. Dickens thought this was extremely cruel. Many people at that time believed poor people were bad people. Through his writing Dickens showed they might have been unlucky or had simply been born poor.

## Children

Dickens felt strongly that children of poor people had particularly bad lives. They became ill, had to work and couldn't go to school. He thought that this was very unfair. He also believed that education would help people have better lives. From 1880, all children between 5 and 10 had to go to school in England.

In Victorian England, what was a poorhouse?
_____

How are poor people helped in modern Britain?
_____

What happened to British children in 1880?
_____

# It's Christmas!

In *A Christmas Carol* we get a very strong idea of what Dickens loved about this big celebration. It was a time for families to be together, eat and have fun. Every journey Scrooge makes with the three ghosts shows us people celebrating together.

Through this, and through the horrible idea of dying alone, Scrooge begins to understand the importance of other people to having a happy and good life.

Christmas puddin

## Food at Christmas

Many homes in Victorian England did have an oven where they could cook their Christmas dinner. Scrooge and the Ghost of Christmas Present watch how the poor use bakers' ovens to cook theirs! People in Victorian England ate turkey, chicken and goose. Today most people in the UK eat turkey at Christmas. The meal ends with the Christmas pudding made from dried fruit, sugar, flour, fat and eggs and cooked in hot water. Today, most people buy their Christmas puddings from the supermarket, but it's easy to make at home!

## Christmas Carols

There are many traditional British songs sung at Christmas. These are called carols, and some are hundreds of years old. Here is an old favourite (which you can find on YouTube).

*We wish you a Merry Christmas; We wish you a Merry Christmas; We wish you a Merry Christmas and a Happy New Year.*
*Good tidings* (news) *we bring to you and your kin* (family and friends)*; We wish you a Merry Christmas and a Happy New Year.*
*Oh, bring us a figgy* (fruit/Christmas) *pudding; Oh, bring us a figgy pudding; Oh, bring us a figgy pudding and a cup of good cheer.*
*We won't go until we get some; We won't go until we get some; We won't go until we get some, so bring some out here.*
*We wish you a Merry Christmas; We wish you a Merry Christmas; We wish you a Merry Christmas and a Happy New Year.*

# Scrooge McDuck and Other Scrooges

**Many films have been made of *A Christmas Carol*. The first film of Scrooge's story was made in 1901.**

## Scrooge McDuck

Scrooge McDuck was created by Carl Barks while working for the Walt Disney Company. Scrooge McDuck is a rich duck, uncle to Donald Duck. He began life as a poor boy in Glasgow, cleaning shoes for rich people. Then he moved to America, found gold in California and became very rich. At first, Scrooge McDuck was like Ebenezer, but he soon began to have adventures around the world. Now he speaks several foreign languages but he isn't always good and he is 'careful' with his money!

## The First Film

It's called *Scrooge*, or *Marley's ghost*, and is a silent film in black and white and is only 6 minutes long. It even has a clever way of showing Marley's face in Scrooge's door. You can watch the whole film on Wikipedia.

## Bah! Humbug

This famous phrase is still used in modern English and for the same reasons that Scrooge used it! We also say that someone who keeps tight hold of their money is 'a Scrooge'.

## Tiny Tim

Tiny Tim only appears once in the story but he is as important as Scrooge himself. 'God bless us, everyone!' is another phrase which is still remembered and repeated in modern English.

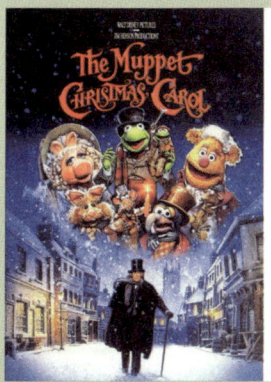

## The Best Scrooges on film

- A musical *Christmas Carol* was made in 1970, with Albert Finney as Scrooge and Alec Guinness as Marley's ghost.
- *The Muppet Christmas Carol* (1992), had Michael Caine as Scrooge, Kermit the Frog as Bob Cratchit and Miss Piggy as Mrs Cratchit.
- *A Christmas Carol* went digital and 3D in 2009, with Jim Carrey as Scrooge and all three ghosts!

# TEST YOURSELF

**Answer these true or false questions**

|   |   | T | F |
|---|---|---|---|
| 1 | At the beginning of this story, Scrooge is sad and lonely. | ☐ | ☐ |
| 2 | Scrooge thinks Bob Cratchit is stealing from him because he wants a day off on Christmas Day. | ☐ | ☐ |
| 3 | Scrooge doesn't spend money on other people, but he spends money on himself. | ☐ | ☐ |
| 4 | Scrooge only starts to believe Marley's ghost is real when he shakes his chain and unwraps his head. | ☐ | ☐ |
| 5 | Marley has travelled the earth since he died, now he has come to tell Scrooge what it is like to be dead. | ☐ | ☐ |
| 6 | The Ghost of Christmas Past has come to help Scrooge remember the past. | ☐ | ☐ |
| 7 | The young Scrooge finds a much happier world in his books. | ☐ | ☐ |
| 8 | The young Scrooge lived at his school all year, until his sister, Fan, comes to bring him home. | ☐ | ☐ |
| 9 | Scrooge watches Fezziwig's party calmly and in silence. | ☐ | ☐ |
| 10 | Scrooge learns about the life of the poor with the Ghost of Christmas present. | ☐ | ☐ |
| 11 | The Ghost of Christmas Yet to Come moves along the ground like fog. | ☐ | ☐ |
| 12 | Scrooge understands immediately that the dead man is himself. | ☐ | ☐ |
| 13 | Scrooge buys a turkey for the Cratchits but doesn't visit them on Christmas Day. | ☐ | ☐ |
| 14 | Scrooge's nephew and his wife take some time to get used to the new Scrooge. | ☐ | ☐ |

# SYLLABUS

## Nouns
Complex noun phrases

## Pronouns
Reflexive and emphatic: *myself*, etc

## Adjectives
Quantitative: *some, any, many, much, a few, a lot of, all, other, every, etc*
Comparative and superlative forms (regular and irregular), *(not) as...as*

## Adverbs
Sentence adverbs: *too, either*, etc.

## Prepositions
Prepositions following nouns and adjectives

## Connectives
*since, as, for, so that, (in order) to, so, so...that, although, while*

## Verb tenses
Present Continuous: future plans and activities
Past Perfect Simple: narrative, reported speech
Future with *will*: offers, promises, predictions, etc

## Verb forms and patterns
Verb + object + full infinitive (e.g. *I want you to go.*)
Verb + object + infinitive
give/take/send/bring/show + direct/indirect object
Phrasal verbs/verbs with prepositions
Conditional sentences: Type 0, 1 and 2
Simple reported speech: statements, questions and commands with *say, ask, tell*
Interrogatives: *what, what* + *noun, where, when, who, which, how much, why*

## Modal verbs
*could*: possibility
*should* (present and future reference): advice
*might* (present and future reference): possibility
*used to + infinitive* (past habits)

## Types of clause
Defining relative clauses with *which, that*, zero pronoun
Time clauses introduced by *when, while, until, before, after, as soon as*
Clauses of purpose: *(in order) to* (infinitive of purpose)

# YOUNG ADULT  READERS

**STAGE 1**    Jonathan Swift, *Gulliver's Travels*
Sir Arthur Conan Doyle, *The Hound of the Baskervilles*
Daniel Defoe, *Robinson Crusoe*

**STAGE 2**    Charles Dickens, *Great Expectations*
William Shakespeare, *Romeo and Juliet*
Bram Stoker, *Dracula*
William Shakespeare, *A Midsummer Night's Dream*
Robert Louis Stevenson, *The Strange Case of Dr Jekyll and Mr Hyde*
Jerome K. Jerome, *Three Men in a Boat*
John Buchan, *Thirty-Nine Steps*

**STAGE 3**    Charlotte Brontë, *Jane Eyre*
Jane Austen, *Pride and Prejudice*
Oscar Wilde, *The Picture of Dorian Gray*
William Shakespeare, *Macbeth*
Jane Austen, *Sense and Sensibility*
Edith Wharton, *The Age of Innocence*
Charles Dickens, *A Christmas Carol*

**STAGE 4**    James Joyce, *Dubliners*
Mary Shelley, *Frankenstein*
Henry James, *The Turn of the Screw*
Emily Brontë, *Wuthering Heights*
Edgar Allan Poe, *Stories of Mystery and Suspense*
Charles and Mary Lamb, *Tales from Shakespeare*
Charles Dickens, *A Tale of Two Cities*
Anthony Hope, *The Prisoner of Zenda*
Hermann Melville, *Moby Dick*
George Eliot, *The Mill on the Floss*

**STAGE 5**    Virginia Woolf, *Mrs Dalloway*
Francis Scott Fitzgerald, *The Great Gatsby*
William Makepeace Thackeray, *Vanity Fair*

**STAGE 6**    Joseph Conrad, *Heart of Darkness*
J. Borsbey & R. Swan, Editors, *A Collection of First World War Poetry*
Oscar Wilde, *The Importance of Being Earnest*

# YOUNG ADULT  READERS (LIGHT)

Edgar Allan Poe, *The Narrative of Arthur Gordon Pym of Nantucket*
Natsume Sōseki, *Botchan*